*To the universe: draw your swords*

# Chapter One

*You only get one chance.* Ever heard that saying?

It's true. Especially with the important things in life. So when that one chance rolls around, you can't afford to screw it up.

Except, somehow, I did.

Things had been going so well between Lindsay and me. After years of just being friends, something had shifted in the way I felt about her. I didn't want to be just friends anymore. And I could kind of tell she didn't either. You know, from the way she looked at me. The way she talked to me. The way we suddenly felt shy with each other when we hadn't before. The way my heart kind of skipped a beat when her name came up on my phone.

It took me months, but I had finally worked up the courage to ask Lindsay out. I had it all planned: I was going to ask her at the year-end party at Sara's place.

On the night of the party, I was nervous as hell. Which is stupid, really, because it's what both of us wanted. But still, you want to do things right, you know?

So anyway, after a few beers everyone was down at the fire pit, and just

Lindsay and I were left sitting on the back deck. It was a cool night in late June. Pink clouds. Still air. The universe had even arranged some lightning flashing on the horizon. Perfect.

Lindsay was lounging on a chaise. I was hanging out on the double swing. She shivered a little. My cue.

"Want my hoodie?"

She smiled and shook her head. "I'm okay." But then she rubbed her arms. Cue number two.

I patted the seat beside me. "Come sit," I said. I held up a corner of the blanket that was draped over the swing back. I could easily have tossed it to her. But that wasn't the point. I wanted her close to me. I couldn't exactly ask her out if she was, like, ten feet away.

Sharing a swing with my best friend was something I would've done without thinking twice just a few months ago. We would have sat together under the

3

blanket and listened to the sounds of laughter drifting up from the fire pit below. Laughed at how drunk other people were. Made fun of teachers we didn't like.

But when it actually *means* something…it's different.

She shrugged. "Sure," she said. "It *is* getting chilly." She stood up. Stretched. God, how had I spent all these years not wanting her? She moved toward the swing. "Shove your butt over, Mikey." I grinned and she sat down beside me. Kicked off her sandals and brought her legs up under her—those long gymnastics-ripped legs of hers. I handed her some blanket and she tucked her feet underneath. She leaned into me. "This okay?"

My stomach did a flip-flop. "Yep." Definitely okay. I took a deep breath. "So," I began. But then I didn't know what else to say. My mind was blank.

Lindsay looked up at me. "Yeah?" The lightning forked a little bit closer. The storm was still too far away for us to hear any thunder. "So?"

"Yeah. That's, uh, that's some pretty great lightning, you know?" I sounded like an idiot.

She put her head on my shoulder. "It's totally great lightning, Mike," she agreed. I heard the smile in her voice.

I got a grip on myself and tried again. I was going to do this. "Yeah, so, um, I wanted to ask you something," I said. I lifted a strand of her hair and wrapped it around my fingers. So soft.

"Mm-hmm?" she asked. "What's that?" Her arm drifted across my stomach and rested there. She never used to do *that*. She hooked her thumb in one of my belt loops. I took another deep breath and let it out slow. Real slow.

"Yeah, so, I was wondering…" Another deep breath. A flash of lightning lit up the horizon. Another followed right on its heels. A puff of wind flipped up the corner of the blanket, exposing Lindsay's legs. Her amazing endless legs. She reached down absently and flicked it back into place. Snugged up tighter to me.

"You were wondering…?"

And suddenly I just…chickened out. "Yeah, I was wondering…do you, uh, do you want…another beer?" I finished lamely. As soon as the words left my mouth, I was furious with myself.

"No," I said, backpedaling. "I mean, never mind. Never mind the beer." I sucked in another breath. "I actually meant to ask you if—"

Right then, Aaron and Morgan crashed through the back door. Lindsay shifted, sitting up and edging over to the other end of the swing.

Morgan had a shaggy beard strapped to his head. He danced over to us in tight yellow Speedos and huge sunglasses, singing "Bohemian Rhapsody."

Normally I would laugh—who wouldn't? The guy's an idiot. But Morgan's screwing around was the last thing I needed right now.

Aaron's eyes lit up when he saw me. "Hey! Whassup, Mikey!!" he shouted. He raised his beer. "You too cool for the rest of us down at the fire pit?"

Just then he noticed Lindsay bunched up at the other end of the swing. He looked from me to her, then back at me. Raised his eyebrows.

I rolled my eyes: *Duh!* Aaron's eyes widened in sudden understanding.

He started to back away. "Du-u-ude," he said. "It's cool. We're leaving now." He punched Morgan on the arm and nodded toward us.

Morgan opened his mouth to speak.

"Shut it," said Aaron. "We're leaving." They turned to go.

But it was too late. The door opened again and a group of girls giggled out onto the porch. More people followed.

And my chance was lost.

# Chapter Two

Lindsay hopped down from the swing. Weaved her way through the group and went into the house. I waited, thinking she had just gone to get another beer.

After about ten minutes, I wondered if she had left. Some people had been talking about going over to Angad's place. Maybe she had gone along?

I didn't go after her. I was too pissed off with myself. Embarrassed too.

I stayed in the semidarkness of the swing, avoiding everyone. Eventually, they drifted across the yard. Back to the fire pit.

Except for Scarlett. She came back after everyone else left.

Everyone at our school knows Scarlett. And every school has one. She's the flirty knockout with a rep for being easy. People call her Skanky Scarlett. I've heard she'll hook up with anyone. Not exactly my type.

She sat down where Lindsay had been only minutes before. She pressed her skinny body against mine, chattering away. Stuff I couldn't care less about. How her skirt shrank in the dryer. How she painted daisies on her nails last night. How she liked to watch my lacrosse games.

I responded just enough to be polite. I was still stewing over fumbling the ball with Lindsay. How could I have choked so badly?

Listening to Scarlett's yapping kind of brought it home. I had to try again. I couldn't let this day end without doing what I'd spent the last five months working up to.

I decided to go after Lindsay. Wherever she was—here or at Angad's place—I wanted to see this thing through.

Lightning flashed. Still no rain, but I could hear the thunder now. The wind was picking up.

"God, it's really cold, eh?" Scarlett was saying. "I'll bet *you* can warm me up, Mike." She shivered prettily and climbed up on my lap. Uh, no. I put my hands on her hips to shove her off. She grabbed my hemp necklace.

"Oh, this is so cool, Mike!" Scarlett squealed. "Can I wear it?" She pulled me closer. I could smell booze on her breath.

Gross.

"I don't think so," I said. I started to push her off.

Then—still holding tight to my necklace—she kissed me.

Right then, Lindsay banged through the back door. "Holy smokes, Mike, you should have seen the lightning from up on the roof—"

She stopped short when she caught sight of me. A beer beside me, Scarlett in my lap, my hands on her hips.

Lindsay's eyes widened. Her lips parted and I heard the breath leave her body like she'd been kicked.

I threw Scarlett off my lap and stood up.

"No. Linds," I said. I spread my hands. Shook my head. "No. This isn't...it's not...I didn't—"

But she didn't stay to listen.

She turned and yanked open the door, one hand covering her mouth.

And then she was gone.

"Lindsay!" I shouted. Out of the corner of my eye, I saw Scarlett slink away.

There was no way I'd ever be able to explain this.

# Chapter Three

Lindsay and I were supposed to have spent the summer together. Watching movies and going on walks. Sitting by the lake late into the night. You know. Parking.

But after that night, she was as good as gone. She didn't give me a chance to explain. I tried texting her from the party to explain. I wrote it and erased it three times. The words wouldn't work. It just sounded like I was trying to cover something up. So I called, but she didn't answer.

I called a couple of more times that night. Straight to voicemail.

I had to admit, the optics were pretty crappy. I wasn't sure whether I could make her believe me.

After that night, she packed up and took off to her grandparents' resort on Chilver Lake. She'd spent summer vacations there before, helping out around the marina. Usually she went for a couple of weeks.

This time, she was gone for the entire summer.

I called a few times during those first days after the train wreck. I didn't want to try to explain anything in an email.

She didn't answer. I was hoping she'd come around and maybe call me, or ask me to come down and help out on the long weekend like I had in other years. But she never did.

My summer sucked. I spent my days slinging bundles of newspapers in the hot warehouse. Loading up the delivery vans. I didn't want to see anyone from school. I missed hanging out with Lindsay. And I felt terrible for hurting her. But I figured we'd work it out when school started up in September.

All I had to do was to get her alone. And explain.

But now that school's back in, talking to Lindsay seems more impossible than ever.

I hardly know who she is now. When she walked into homeroom at the start of the year, I barely recognized her. Last spring, she was this kick-ass athlete with a super soft side. She cried once when she forgot her grandpa's birthday. Another time it was because a dragonfly hit the windshield.

Now that she's back...I don't know. She's gone from lululemon and flip-flops to short skirts and monster heels that could spear you with one kick. She's thinner and blonder. Wearing tiny clothes. Showing a lot of skin. She's smoking too. Hanging around with the popular girls outside at lunchtime.

Her new BFFs. Although you can hardly call them friends. It's a constant battle between them to see who's got the best labels, who's got the coolest nails, who ate the tiniest amount at their last meal. It's stupid. But ever since the start of school, Lindsay has been hanging with that group. She must see something in them. I don't know what though.

It's hard to imagine approaching this new version of Lindsay. I don't feel like trying to wade into her little group of frenemies. How intimidating is *that*?

It's weird that so much can change between two people so quickly. I mean, until a few months ago, Lindsay and I were pretty much inseparable. We spent countless Friday nights eating popcorn and watching movies. Talking about stuff. The guys she liked. The girls I dated. She used to tease me that I went through girls faster than a Super G racer through the slalom gates.

That was before I realized the only one I wanted was her.

We texted constantly. Nowadays, my mom is the person I text the most. It's depressing.

Lacrosse is back in full swing now too. Sometimes I see Scarlett sitting on the sidelines with a group of her friends. Watching. She's probably got her sleaze radar set on some other guy. Maybe I should make *her* explain to Lindsay what happened.

I consider this as Ms. Weston drones on about molarity. I hate chemistry. I hate pretty much everything these days.

Ms. Weston's back is turned and she's writing on the board. She's sporting one of her famous wedgies, her pants riding up between her big square bum cheeks. The Weston Wedgie, we call it. As if he can read my mind, Morgan nudges my foot with his sneaker. He nods toward Ms. Weston's butt. He winks and runs his tongue along his lips. I crack up.

"Somebody have something to share?" says Ms. Weston without turning around.

No one answers. The Wedgie goes on writing. "Get this all down in your books, folks," she says. We dutifully copy formulas. Out of habit, I glance over to where Lindsay is sitting, two rows away. She's actually here today, which is rare. She's been blowing off classes lately. Probably smoking out by the dumpsters. Or maybe shopping.

My heart stops for a second. She's looking right at me. Before I can figure out whether I should smile, she looks away. Tosses her blond hair. Mad that I caught her expression.

But I caught it, all right. That was the old Lindsay looking at me. One side of her mouth turned up in the hint of a smile. She knew why I was laughing.

I look back at the board and sigh, picking up my pen. What the hell? That's not the first time I've caught Lindsay looking at me. I mean, I stare at *her* all the time, but that's because she's, like, the center of my universe. She's always frosty to me now, but I can't just erase seven years of liking someone. And one year of being in love with them.

I wonder whether she really hates me. When I catch her looking at me like that, it sure doesn't look like she hates me. But then when she sees me looking at her, she goes all Ice Queen again. Sometimes she'll turn and say something to her friends and they'll laugh. It bothers me. But I'd have to be an idiot to show it.

I decide to talk to her today. I don't care how scary it's going to be to break in on her little gaggle of girlfriends. I need to explain to her what happened.

## Chapter Four

By lunchtime, I'm nervous again at the thought of barging in and stealing Lindsay away from the Perfect Girls. It's a warm September day, and they're all sitting on the grass outside. I pull my phone out of my pocket. Toss my sub wrapper into a garbage can near the window where I'm spying on them.

Morgan strolls by, singing. He's wearing a girl's field-hockey skirt. A blue bra stretches across his T-shirt. He must have lost a bet or something. Then again, this is Morgan we're talking about.

He pulls his earbuds out and comes to stand at the window. He looks out at the group of girls sprawled on the lawn. "Buncha hotties right there," he says.

"Yeah."

"Lindsay's smokin' now, eh?" he says. "She's turned into a real good-time girl. Totally different than she was last year."

I clear my throat and look down at my phone. "Yep." I don't feel like talking about this with Morgan. What does he know about Lindsay? I start punching in my message.

"So did you guys ever, uh…you know?" Morgan wiggles his eyebrows at me and nods his head in Lindsay's direction. "Last summer?"

I jerk my head up and look at him. "What's it to you?" It comes out harder than I mean it to.

Morgan raises his palms to me in mock surrender. "Hey, homes, I'm just asking." He glances out the window and lowers his voice. "I hear she's good."

I stare at him. This conversation, like his outfit, has just turned surreal. Is he saying Lindsay has a rep? As far as I know, Lindsay has never been with a guy in her life.

"Is that what you hear." I don't say it as a question. I force my expression to stay neutral.

Morgan lifts one eyebrow. "You should know, man."

But I don't know, that's the thing. Much as I wish I might, I don't.

"Who's talking?" I ask.

"Benson," he answers. "Says they hooked up at the dance last Friday."

Mark Benson. One of the senior football thugs. Charming guy. Popular, but who the hell knows why. He looks like Shrek. As far as I know, Lindsay doesn't even know him. So what the hell's she going after him for? This can't be right. Morgan's talking crazy.

It's like he's reading my mind. "You didn't know? They're all into it." He jerks his head toward the girls on the lawn. "It's, like, this contest they've got going. To see which of them can get the most guys. You know." He shrugs. "Oral."

All the air leaves my body. He's wrong. He's got to be wrong. This Mark guy is going around spreading rumors about Lindsay. She would never in a million years be in on something like that.

"And you know about this how?" I ask.

"Renata," Morgan says simply. A wicked grin spreads across his face. "Now that one...*she*'s a live wire."

Suddenly I want to punch him. I turn to the window so I don't have to look at him. How have I not known about this? I look at Lindsay sitting on the lawn, next to Renata and Erin. The sun shines on her carefully styled hair. I remember how soft it felt when I was holding her on the swing at Sara's place. When it was just loose and natural, tumbling over her shoulders.

It feels like that was ten years ago.

I close my eyes. I feel sick at the game she's playing. I mean, I'm not stupid: I know it happens. I even know other girls who do that kind of thing at this school. Jesus, some of them have even asked *me*. The Lindsay I know would never have made a game out of it, never given it away like that to someone who didn't mean anything to her. Christ, before the summer she never even *did* that stuff. I know it for a fact, just like I knew pretty much everything about her.

I wonder what else I don't know now. How did she change so much in just one summer?

Morgan's words pull me out of my thoughts. There's a question in his voice, and I hate it. "So, you know, uh, if you and Lindsay aren't actually together, is she—?"

I open my eyes and look at him. "You should shut up," I say.

Morgan takes a little step backward. His hands come up again. He looks at me warily. "Hey, Mike," he says. "No hard feelings, man. It's cool. I don't need—it's not a big thing." He shrugs. "It's cool."

Slowly, I release the breath I've been holding. "Right," I say. "It's cool."

Morgan nods. "Okay." He gives me a light punch on the shoulder. Puts his earbuds back in and straightens his bra. "I'll see you at practice."

As soon as he's gone, I type in my message to Lindsay. Until a few minutes ago, I was nervous about this. But what I've just learned skips me right over any feelings of awkwardness. I need to talk to Lindsay. Now.

**U busy? Can u talk?**

I duck my head a bit, watching through the window. She takes out her phone and looks at it. She stares at the screen for a moment and then puts the phone down. Damn. She's going to ignore me.

I feel stupid. Now I'm glad I didn't take a chance on trying to talk with her in person. I would have had to suffer being rejected in front of all those… rejects she calls her friends.

I see Morgan come out the main doors and saunter over to the group of girls on the grass. They laugh and catcall at his skirt. He grabs the bra in his hands and massages his chest. The girls giggle again. I watch as he grabs Sareena's leg, tickling her until she squeals and moves over so he can sit down. It's something I would have done, before all this. Now I'm way too edgy. Too self-conscious around Lindsay and the little posse that's adopted her.

Maybe I shouldn't care so much. Maybe I should just…get over it. There are plenty of other fish in the ocean. Right?

Right.

Except no one else really interests me. Just Lindsay.

But now I know she obviously isn't interested. Not in me, at least.

Yeah, maybe I should just…let it go.

I straighten up and look out the window again. Lindsay looks away from the group. I see her draw a big breath in.

She picks up her phone and my heart does a crazy little double-skip. *Let it go?* I almost laugh. What am I thinking? I can't let this thing go. This girl has my heart in her hands. She always has.

She bends her head over her phone and types. Renata leans in and says something. Lindsay smiles faintly. Then she looks up and sighs. God, I feel like a stalker. Spying on her through the window. My phone vibrates and I jump. I look at the screen.

**Busy now. Hanging with the girls. What's up?**

*What's up?* Two words. So casual.

But they're the first words I've had from her in months.

Seeing her message hits me like a bolt of lightning. My face goes hot. My ears start to burn.

I didn't know what I was expecting. But apparently I wasn't expecting her to answer me. I look at my phone again.

**What's up?**

*What's up? Jesus, Lindsay. I miss you and I'm worried about you and I want to talk to you. And I love you. That's what's up.*

But that's not what I say. I look back through the window. Sara and Renata are talking with Morgan. Lindsay's not listening though. She's pulled her knees up to her chest and wrapped her arms around them.

I begin to type. Fast, before I second-guess myself. **Want to meet after practice? Done at 4.**

I hit Send and watch.

She picks up her phone. Reads my message. She looks off across the playing field.

She's thinking. This is good.

Then she starts to gather up her things, stuffing them into her bag. I can see her telling the others that she's heading out.

Worried that she might see me at the window, I turn and head downstairs. I'll go to my locker and grab my books for the afternoon. Turn things over in my mind.

I'm spinning the combination on my lock when my phone buzzes. I drop the lock and grab my phone. My stomach sinks.

**Sorry. Going out with Stefano after school.**

No *How about tomorrow?* or *Call me later.* Just this.

Well, what did I expect? It's been months since we even so much as texted each other. And here I am hoping she's ready to be friends again. As if.

And who the hell is this Stefano guy? The only Stefano I know of is in grade twelve, and he's a dick. Is she going to…add him to the contest too?

I shake my head. Why did I even bother sending her a message?

I jerk my locker open and grab my history binder. Whatever. Lindsay can have her fun with this guy. She can play her stupid games with her stupid friends. I'm done. Putting her out of my mind.

Moving on.

# Chapter Five

I'm about to throw my equipment bag over my shoulder when my phone vibrates. It's probably Mom, telling me to pick something up for dinner on my way home.

I reach for my phone.

It's Lindsay. My breath catches in my throat. Wow.

**Hey. WRU?**

Last week's decision to put her out of my mind disappears.

**Leaving the field**, I type. **We kicked ass**. I grin as I replay the winning goal in my mind's eye. A tiebreaker delivered by Jamal, and assisted by me.

**Good boi. U r a star. Lacrosse again next yr?**

I flush, my face growing hot. My eyes linger on *boi* and *star*. I like those words. Especially from her. And I like how she's asking about my plans for next year.

Yeah, of course I'll play again next year. I love this game.

**Yep**. I decide to ask her what I've been wondering about. **You going to the party next Fri?** She'll probably be there. After all, it's at Erin's house. But I want to know for sure. We don't ever communicate at school—except for those don't-catch-me-looking-at-you looks. But maybe it would be different at a party. Maybe it would be easier to hang out and talk with loud music playing and people shouting all around us.

**Duh, silly. Erin's my BFF—course I'll go. You?**

I smile at her calling me silly. She might be all slick-chick hot on the outside, but she's still pure Linds on the inside. I reply. **After work.**

Before she can respond, I start typing again. **U busy l8r? Want to watch a show?** I'd way rather spend Monday night watching a movie with Lindsay than finish that lame socials essay. I cross my fingers that she'll ditch her pedicure or whatever in favor of lying around eating popcorn instead. It would be just like old times.

*Buzz*. **Na. At Rob's. Hot tub. So good**.

I swallow. Who's Rob? I stare at the words on the screen for what feels like an eternity.

*Hot tub.* My chest tightens. Why is she texting me with this crap? Does she really think I want to know what she's doing with other guys?

*So good.*

I want to scream and throw the phone across the field.

Instead, I type: **Sounds fun. Enjoy that**. I punch Send and stuff my phone back into my pocket. Screw you, Lindsay, I think. I'm done with you and your stupid little mind games.

I'm left standing alone on the edge of the field. My earlier excitement at having won the game is gone. I'm suddenly tired. Tired of thinking about Lindsay. Tired of worrying about her only to turn around and get kicked in the stomach again.

Tired of everything.

I feel a pinch on my elbow and turn my arm to find a mosquito bleeding me dry. Figures. I squeeze my skin for a few seconds, trapping his little sucker so he can't get away. Then I slap him. He explodes in a splatter of blood across my arm.

Nice.

Sighing, I heave my heavy bag over my shoulder and trudge off across the grass toward home.

# Chapter Six

I stuff a sheaf of flyers into the last news-paper and throw it onto the pile. That's a wrap. I've done about a thousand today. My hands are black and inky. Gross.

I say goodnight to Ken and hop in the truck. I'll clean up at home.

Mom greets me as I drop my keys on the front table. "Hi, baby. How was your day?" She's already eaten supper and is settling in to her evening routine. She's curled up on the sofa with a couple of magazines. Babs is snuggled into her leg, purring like a chainsaw that's running out of gas.

"All right," I say. "Got a seventy-six on my bio midterm. And seventy-eight in English."

"Nice work." She smiles. "You have plans for tonight?" She strokes Babs behind the ears.

"Yeah, there's a party at this girl's place. Erin," I say.

A frown creases her forehead. "Where does she live? Are you driving?"

I shake my head. "I can walk. It's only twenty minutes."

Her face relaxes. "That's good. But you should eat before you go, honey." She's right. I should. Beer on an empty stomach is a recipe for stupid stuff. "And take your phone with you."

"Kay." I peel off my socks and throw them at the laundry basket.

"Who all's going to be there? Any parents?"

I shrug.

Mom sighs. "I figured as much," she says. "Any friends I know?"

"Morgan. Aaron." I pause. "Lindsay."

"Mmm," she says. "I love that Morgan boy. He is such a character. You should have him over sometime." She looks at me over the top of her glasses. "I haven't seen much of Lindsay lately. How is she these days?"

I shrug again. "Okay, I guess." I don't want to get into it right now. I'm starving, I'm dirty, I smell like an ink factory, and it's already almost 8:00 PM.

I head for the bathroom. "I'm shower-ing," I call over my shoulder.

Forty-five minutes later I'm on Erin's doorstep. Jamal and Neil arrive at the same time, which makes for an easy entrance. The music shakes the whole house. I don't bother to ring the bell. No one'll hear it. We step inside.

"Smoking outside *ONLY*!" shrieks a familiar voice. I watch as Renata shoos two girls out onto the side deck. She takes a sip from the glass in her hand and surveys the room. Such a boss.

She sees me. A big smile breaks across her face. "Well, if it isn't Mister Lacrosse Star himself!" She sidles over. Stares up at me from under long black lashes. I roll my eyes. What a faker. "Where have you *been*? Mike Mullens,

you have been a *stranger* lately."
Even though I know she's playing me,
I let her. I need some girl attention.

Renata grabs my arm. She pulls me
into the kitchen and opens the fridge.
Thrusts a beer into my hand. "There.
*Now* the night can start." As soon as she
says the words, she's gone. Off to douse
some other fire, no doubt.

I look around me. It's less crowded
in the kitchen than in the living room.
People are standing around, talking and
laughing. A few girls sit on the counter-
tops, drinking.

One of them is Lindsay.

My stomach gives a little lurch when
I see her. When she looks my way,
I raise my bottle slightly. She smiles
back before remembering that she's
supposed to be cold. Her smile turns
into a sort of half sneer. She turns her
head and goes back to talking to Erin.

A hand slips into my back pocket and I turn. Morgan squeezes my butt and coos, "Oh, Mike Mullens. Where have you *been*? You *stranger*!" I laugh. Morgan grabs another beer and goes back to the living room, singing "Sesame Street."

I glance back at Lindsay. She looks incredible. She's got on a tiny denim skirt and a pink T-shirt. Toes painted to match. Killer.

She's laughing now at something Erin is saying. Watching her makes me ache. How did I screw it up so badly last spring? Why am I standing here, staring at her, miles away from being able to start a conversation? Why isn't she laughing at something *I'm* saying?

She's holding a tall bottle in her hand. When she raises it to her lips, I see what it is. Raspberry schnapps. Holy crap. That's deadly stuff. She never used to drink like this. And she's taking it straight. Crazy girl. She's going to be falling-down drunk in no time.

Erin hops down to get another beer. Lindsay sees me watching her. This time she doesn't look away. Instead, she takes another pull on the bottle. Slow. Graphic. In-your-face sexy. Eyes on me the whole time. She lifts her chin, and I catch a challenge in her eyes.

I'm trying to figure this out when she throws me for another loop by flashing a wicked smile.

Then her eyes shift to look over my shoulder, through the doorway to the living room. I roll my tongue up and tuck it back inside my head before turning. A couple of seniors have just arrived. A case of beer clinks as it's set down on the floor.

Great.

# Chapter Seven

"Josh is here!" Lindsay exclaims. She turns to Erin, who's taken her spot on the countertop again. "He came!" She's slurring her words a little.

Erin squeals in solidarity, although she could care less.

If this is the Josh I'm thinking of, he's the head of the Student Theater Society. Real big man around school.

Everybody knows him from assemblies and school performances. He's the loudest, and the funniest. But he's also the biggest prick of them all.

Lindsay sets down her bottle and hops off the counter. "I'm gonna go say hi," she says as she straightens her skirt. It's so short I can practically see her underwear. She takes a step toward the doorway. Her knees buckle, and she grabs for the counter. Holy. She's plastered, and it's not even nine thirty yet.

"Whoa. Linds." Instinctively I put my arm out to steady her. This close, she smells of raspberries. And vanilla.

"I'm fine," she says, louder than she needs to. But her hand is on my arm. She looks up at me. A long, searching look.

She holds my gaze for what feels like forever. It hits me that this is a good time to try to talk to her. Right here, in the middle of this busy, noisy kitchen, with five other people around us and a constant stream of fridge traffic.

I've been looking for the right moment. And I'm tired of waiting for it to show up.

I take a deep breath. "Linds. There's something I need to—"

Josh's big laugh rings out. It drowns out my words.

And kills the moment.

Lindsay blinks and the veil drops back into place. She lets go of my arm and straightens her shirt. Raises her chin and looks at me with flashing eyes.

"Do you mind, Mike?" she hisses. "You're standing in the doorway."

I step back like I've been scorched. She brushes past me, her breasts skimming my chest on her way through the door.

What was that all about?

Josh laughs again. The noise grates on me. I can hear him booming some joke about girls with fat asses. Boy, Lindsay sure knows how to pick them.

I think about the bottle again. About Lindsay's mouth. On the bottle. The image of her and Josh explodes into my mind. I grit my teeth. Jerk. She's way too good for him.

Suddenly this all seems like something off the back of one of those dumb romance novels my mom reads. I laugh at myself. What an idiot. I fell right into Lindsay's mean little trap. That whole show with the bottle just now? That wasn't a come-on. She just wants to stab me to death for embarrassing her last spring.

She is going to make me pay. Over. And over. And over.

I look into the living room. Lindsay's scooched up next to Josh on the sofa. I watch as her hand snakes out and rests on Josh's thigh. She's smiling up at him, listening intently to whatever bullshit he's spewing out of those thick laughing lips.

I sigh. Maybe I'll snag a chance later. I take the last slug of beer.

"Why so mopey?"

I turn. Sara's watching me.

"Didn't know I was moping." I say.

She considers this. "Maybe not moping. But you're definitely mooning." Her eyes move to the scene on the couch, then back to me.

"Need more beer, I guess." I swirl my empty bottle.

"Atta boy." She grins and opens the fridge. Hands me a bottle. I open it and hand it back to her. Girls hate twisting off those sharp caps. She grabs another one for me.

"Indulge responsibly." She smiles. We clink. Sara's cool. She and Lindsay were pretty good friends up until Lindsay's little social group switcheroo this year.

"I'm going out onto the deck," Sara says. She glances over my shoulder at the crowded living room. People are dancing, making out, playing drinking games. She looks back at me. "You should come too. The interesting people are *out*side." The screen door slams shut behind her.

I look back toward the living room. Lindsay is sitting on Josh's knee now. She's pressed right up against him. He's got one hand on her hip, almost under her skirt. He's drinking a beer with the other. She's smiling, tucking his long Drama Man hair behind his ear and saying something to him.

Part of me wants to leave. Just go outside and talk to some friends and relax a bit. Try to enjoy myself with a girl I like. A different girl.

But another part of me doesn't want to let Lindsay out of my sight. She's hammered, and I'm worried she's going to do something stupid.

But the second I think this, I realize how stupid *I'm* being. Lindsay doesn't need me to look out for her. She wouldn't even want me to now.

Realizing this makes my decision easy. Okay. Fine. I'm going elsewhere.

I'm about to turn and head for the deck when I see Josh's ugly friend Bryce take a little plastic bag out of his pocket. I watch as he opens it up and reaches inside. Takes something out. A tablet. Ecstasy. He passes the bag to Renata, who's stuck to his side. She giggles and takes one. Passes the bag to Josh.

My stomach tightens into a knot. Josh takes a tablet.

He passes the bag to Lindsay. She's so messed she can hardly focus. I send her a silent message. *No, Linds. Don't do it.*

Josh laughs and takes the bag from her. Whispers something in her ear.

She giggles and opens her mouth for him. I can't believe this. Lindsay doesn't even know what she's doing. She's never *ever* taken drugs before. She would never do that with someone she hardly even knows. She's an A student, for god's sake! She—

Josh places the little tablet on her tongue. *NO!*

I realize I can't let Lindsay have that tablet. I take a step toward the doorway.

That's when she turns and looks right at me. My feet freeze to the floor. She smiles dreamily. Opens her mouth and shows me the little blue tablet on her tongue. Then she winks and blows me a kiss.

I shake my head at her and mouth the word *no*.

But she doesn't see it.

Because right then, Josh takes her chin in his hand and turns her face toward him. My heart empties itself of blood in a rush. I stare in hot misery as their lips meet. His hands slide around her hips, pulling her close. She brings her hands up slowly, until she's holding his face. My jaw locks up and I feel an aching in my throat that I haven't felt in years. I rip my eyes away from the scene in front of me and stumble out onto the deck.

I lean on the railing and rest my head on my arms. I close my eyes. Just for a second.

And I wait. For my heart to slow down. For the blood to stop pounding in my ears. For my breathing to return to normal. I wait to be a little less crazy.

I can hear the music from inside. The Black Eyed Peas, telling us all how tonight's going to be a good night.

Right.

Suddenly my head snaps up.

*Shit.*

Lindsay took that pill and I didn't stop her.

# Chapter Eight

I race back inside and look around.

Lindsay is headed up the stairs. She's following Josh, holding his hand.

Unsure of my plan—or whether I even have one—I follow them.

By the time she's walking through the bedroom doorway, I'm right behind her. Josh is already inside. Lindsay turns to close the door. In this unguarded moment, she looks unhappy. She sees me and stares, confused. She looks drunk and messy and tired.

Why is she doing this?

"Lindsay," I begin. What am I going to say? I didn't think about this. I just... ran up here and now I'm standing in her way. Wanting to stop her from doing something stupid.

I reach out and catch her wrist in my hand. I lower my voice. "Linds. Don't go in there. You're drunk. You're on drugs. You don't know what you're doing."

She frowns. A strand of hair has fallen across her face. Impatient, she reaches up and pushes it out of the way. She twists her arm out of my grasp. "What are you doing here, Mike? Can't you see I'm *busy*?" Her words are thick, and she speaks slowly.

I don't want Lindsay in that room, with that guy, tonight. And I don't care how mad she gets at me for intervening. I know exactly what she's got planned.

And I also know that she's wasted. Maybe she just means to add another little notch in her belt to tell her girlfriends about. But who's to say it'll stop there? What if they decide to take it even farther? Even though Lindsay has been putting on a good show of being a different person than she used to be, I'm convinced she hasn't changed in every way.

I'm certain she hasn't slept with anyone yet. We talked about it more than once. She told me she was waiting for the right time—and the right guy. The old Lindsay would never have pissed something like that away with some stoner at a party.

I look into Lindsay's face. God, she's pretty. Even when she's all smudgy and mad. I take a deep breath. "I need to talk to you. Now. It's important." I pause. "And it's long overdue."

Something flickers in her eyes. She looks down at her hands. I see a muscle working in her jaw. Then she looks back up at me.

I'm surprised by how cold her voice is.

"I don't think so, Mike," she says. "You've had lots of time to talk to me." Anger flashes in her eyes. "And last I checked, you had a lot of explaining to do."

Josh appears in the doorway behind her. He slides his hand around her stomach and looks at me. He's trying to figure out what's going on.

Suddenly Lindsay's tone changes, growing sweet. But her words are bitter. "What's the matter, Mikey? You jealous?" She pulls her shirt up, revealing a beautiful slice of gymnastics-toned stomach.

Her chin dips down and she looks at me through flirty lashes. "You want a piece of me?" She traces a finger slowly from my collarbone to my belt.

The she laughs, big, openmouthed, loud. She pushes me, hard. Caught off guard, I take a step backward.

Her eyes narrow. "You had your chance, Mike." Her words sting me like a slap in the face. Without taking her eyes off me, she grabs Josh's hand and pushes it up, slowly, under her shirt. He smirks, sliding the other hand under too. My jaw tenses and my hands draw themselves into fists.

*Breathe*, I tell myself.

I hear a noise behind me and turn. Bryce is edging past me, heading into the bedroom.

With Lindsay and Josh.

What the hell? What's *he* going in there for? This scene is getting even sketchier. *Two* guys? I don't like this at all.

I don't want Bryce going into that room. I raise my arm to block him. But he's fast for a drama queen. He grabs my arm and twists it behind my back, jamming me face-first into the side of the door. Josh pushes Lindsay behind him into the room. She stumbles. The door closes. Bryce and I are left on the outside.

Suddenly I'm angry. Really angry. Who does this dick think he is? I bounce off the door frame and grab him again. He throws my hands off. With a solid crunch, he slams his shoulder into my chest and sends me flying. I grab for the railing at the top of the stairway, but my hands slice through air, catching nothing. My feet stumble and miss, failing me. I feel myself pinwheeling backward.

Down the stairs.

# Chapter Nine

I come to in a haze of light and noise. I remember falling.

My head hurts. It's resting in someone's lap. I hear sirens.

No. Not sirens. Screaming.

No, that's not screaming. It's singing.

It's Renata. She's singing at the top of her lungs. "Bad Romance." In a really bad voice. She pauses after every verse to take a drag off her cigarette. Looks like she's done with being the smoke police for the night.

I guess I'm not dead, then, because I'm pretty sure Renata's not supposed to be in my version of heaven.

The music booms. I hear bottles clinking and people laughing. Something wet presses on my forehead. Ouch.

Renata notices me looking around and shrieks. It startles me.

"Jesus! What the hell?" I try to sit up, but hands push me down.

Renata shrieks again. *"He's awake!"* Then, as if I can't understand English, she pushes her face close and talks to me slowly, in a loud voice. "Mike, can you hear me? Michael? Can you hear me?"

I try to sit up again. My head is throbbing.

Sara puts a hand on my chest. "Just relax, Mike," she says.

"What happened?" I ask.

"*He speaks!*" screeches Renata. "Mike! You're *alive*! You fell down, like, a *thousand* stairs! You should be dead!"

Sara shoots Renata a look. "Renata. Please."

Renata blinks. "What? Didn't you *see* him? He, like, almost *died*!" She takes a drag off her smoke and blows it at Sara. "He shouldn't even be alive right now." She starts singing again.

I remember Renata helping herself to one of the colorful little tabs that Bryce brought.

Sara ignores her. "You fell down the stairs, Mike. You banged your head pretty good." She shows me the cloth that she's been holding on my forehead. Blood smears one side. "It looks worse than it is," she says. "Mostly you got a really big bump. You're pretty lucky."

"How'd I fall?" I ask. I know for sure I hadn't been drinking enough to actually fall down a flight of stairs. Had I?

Sara shrugs. "No one saw it happen. You just came flying down the stairs. We made sure you were okay, and then we waited for you to come around."

Suddenly I connect all the dots.

Renata.

Bryce.

His bag of tablets.

Josh.

*Lindsay!*

I struggle into a sitting position. Sara sits back on her heels, holding the cloth. She doesn't try to stop me this time. My head gives a sharp throb. "Jesus, Sara. How long have I been passed out?"

She shrugs. "Ten, fifteen minutes?"

Shit. That's a lifetime. Anger knots my chest. Here I've been lying on the carpet like Sleeping Beauty while my best friend gets her brains screwed out by a couple of jackass seniors. Nice work, Mike, I think. You're a real white knight, aren't you?

I look up, toward the top of the stairway. The bedroom door is open a bit. The light's off. Did she leave with those guys?

I push myself up onto my feet and stand. My head hurts. Doesn't matter. I've got to find Lindsay. I touch Sara's shoulder. "Thanks, man."

"Anytime!" chirps Renata.

Sara nods.

Head pounding, I climb the stairs.

I reach the landing and push the door open. It takes my eyes a few seconds to adjust to the darkness. I can just make out the shape on the bed. It's Lindsay. She's alone.

Good. She didn't leave with those guys.

She's not moving.

My relief changes to fear. I hurry to the side of the bed. Hold my hand over her face. My body relaxes when I feel her breath on my palm. But is she hurt? I stretch my fingers out, searching for the switch on the bedside lamp.

I turn the light on and stare.

She's lying on her back, sprawled across the bed.

Naked.

I was too late. Too late to stop those jerks.

Seeing Lindsay like this breaks my heart. The way her lean body looks like a rag doll that's been tossed aside. So disrespected. Her T-shirt is pushed up around her neck. Her bra is off, flung up against the pillows. Her skirt and panties are bunched up on the floor.

Vomit stains the pillow beside her head. The little blue tablet of ecstasy is there too. Thank god. She must've been really sick to spit that up so fast after dropping.

I strip off the dirty pillowcase and throw it on the floor.

I go and close the door, swallowing the sudden lump in my throat. No one else needs to see this.

I begin picking up Lindsay's clothes. This is the first time I've seen her naked since we were little kids. She's beautiful. But it's hardly the way I'd imagined it to be.

I toss her skirt and underwear on the bed and stuff her bra into my pocket. That'll be too hard to get on right. I tug her shirt down until it covers her belly. Next up: underwear. I work them up over her legs and onto her hips.

I slide her jean skirt up and over her legs, straightening it until she looks pretty much decent. She's still passed out, breathing deeply. She hasn't moved since I came in. I reach out and brush her hair off her face.

And suddenly I'm overcome. What's going *on*? How did things get so messed up for my best friend? I rub my hands over my face. A black thought gnaws at the edges of my mind. The thought that, maybe if I hadn't screwed things up so badly back in June, Lindsay and I would be together right now. That maybe she wouldn't have gone away for the whole summer and come back a sleazy guy pleaser who only cares about looking good, being thin and beating her friends at this stupid game they're playing.

That maybe she wouldn't have to wake up and realize she's just lost her virginity to two guys at a party where she was drunk and high on E.

That maybe—if I'd manned up and tried harder to actually straighten out the mess between us—this never would have happened.

## Chapter Ten

I look at the clock: *10:21*. I lie down next to Lindsay, curling my body against hers. I think about how much I've let her down. And then I think about what I can do to make it up to her.

Eventually her steady, deep breathing lulls me to sleep.

I wake up just after midnight. The music is still thumping. Party's going strong. I prop myself up on one elbow. Lindsay is waking up. She moans and opens her eyes. She sees me. Covers her face with one hand.

"Mike," she whispers. "It's you."

I touch her hair.

Without a word, she rolls toward me. I put my arms around her.

"I feel like shit," she says. "Where are we?"

"At Erin's," I answer.

She's quiet for a moment.

"Why are we in the bedroom?" There's dread in her voice.

Briefly, I consider lying to her. Maybe I can save her from herself.

But no. That's not going to work. I can't lie about this.

Choosing my words carefully, I tell her what happened. That she drank, and dropped E, and then took Josh into the bedroom. That Bryce came too. That I tried to stop her, but that she shut me out. I don't tell her that Bryce threw me down the stairs.

"Both of them? Did I…what happened?" She looks up at me. "Josh *and* Bryce? Was it…did they…?" Her voice trails off. Closes her eyes. She can't even finish the question. "Are you sure?"

I nod.

She doesn't want to hear it. "But I'm wearing all my clothes, Mike," she says. Her voice is pleading. It trembles and rises a bit, panicky. "I didn't. They couldn't. Look, see? I'm still wearing all my clothes." She looks up at me desperately.

I smooth her hair off her hot forehead. I wish I could lie, but I can't.

"I got you dressed," I say.

And then she starts to cry.

She cries and cries, and I hold her and try to think of something to say that will make her feel better. But I can't.

When her tears finally run dry, she stays there, face pressed into my shirt, for a long time. Finally she pulls away and wipes the last smudges of makeup from her eyes. Her face is red and blotchy.

She lets out a shaky sigh. "You must think I'm awful," she whispers.

I'm surprised by her words. "Why would I think that?"

She ignores my question. "I never meant for this to happen. I don't know what I meant to happen, but it wasn't this. I never wanted this. I don't care about those"—she shudders—"those losers. None of them. None of them matter to me. They're all jerks."

So all this crap since she came back from summer holidays...there's no point to it? It's all just been for show?

Who is she trying to impress?

"Then why are you doing all this crazy stuff?" I ask. We both know what I'm talking about.

"I don't know," says Lindsay. She sounds defeated. "It's all just so stupid. I guess I was hurt. After you—" She takes a big breath. "After last summer. I was so hurt when I found you and"—she hitches in a big breath—"you and Scarlett. On the swing. I w-w-wanted to show you I didn't care," she says. She hiccups and another sob erupts. "I just w-wanted..." Her voice trails off. "And now you think I'm a s-slut. Because of all this." She starts crying again.

This is the moment I've been waiting for. I need to tell her that it was all just a big mistake. That we've been misunderstanding each other all this time.

That I don't think she's a slut. That I totally, fully, *hugely* want to be with her.

And only her. Not that dumb little tramp, Scarlett. Not anyone. Just Lindsay.

"Linds," I say. I pull away from her a bit so I can look at her. She sniffles and wipes her eyes. She won't look at me.

"Hey." I put my hand under her chin and lift. Her eyes meet mine. They're soft and gray and sad—but I'm about to change that.

I open my mouth to tell her everything that matters.

And that's when the door crashes open.

# Chapter Eleven

Morgan and Aamena. They're laughing, pushing each other. Looking for a place to be alone. By the time they see us and shut each other up with loud *Ssshhhhh* noises and apologize for barging in, the moment is completely destroyed.

I walk Lindsay home. We don't say anything. It's totally strange. She's still pretty tipsy, but she's become hard again, locked up. At half past midnight, I walk her right up to her door. We're ahead of her one o'clock curfew.

I reach out to give her a hug, but she ducks me. I end up giving her an awkward two-handed pat on the back as she steps inside. The door closes and I stand there for a second, unsure how I should feel.

My mind runs on overdrive the whole way home.


By Monday, we're back at school. And Lindsay's walls are still up. She doesn't even look in my direction. I guess she's feeling pretty crappy about what happened at the party. I wonder if she's mad that I didn't fend off those guys. But then I think that's crazy. She didn't even want me there in the first place. Maybe she's ashamed that I found her naked.

Maybe she's pissed that I'm meddling. Maybe she's embarrassed that she said too much.

Maybe I should just chill out and forget about it. Jesus.

At break, I'm headed toward the vending machine—the one that sells good stuff, not all that heart-healthy crap. As I pass a row of lockers, I hear hooting noises. I look over and see Josh-the-drama-dork standing there. He's surrounded by a few guys in his grade. They're all kind of laughing in a weird, quiet way.

I'm curious. And I'll admit to a certain sick urge to find out more about this loser.

I drift over to the group. They're all clustered around, watching something on the cell phone that Josh is holding. I stand a little ways behind them so as not to draw attention to myself. But I can see what they're looking at.

It's video footage of someone having sex with a girl. No audio. Her hair covers her face. It's pretty obvious that she's completely out of it. She's not even moving. Although you can't see his face on the screen, I take it that Josh must be the loverboy, judging from the backslapping and *Whoo*ing that's going on between these guys.

But if Josh is doing all the…um, work…then who's holding the camera? There must be someone else there. That's a bit creepy.

I spy something bright pink on the screen, and that's when I start to put it all together. My mind resists, but I can't stop the pieces of the puzzle from dropping into place.

The bright pink thing is a bra. It's on the bed. It's by the pillows.

Lindsay was wearing a pink bra on the night of Erin's party. *That* pink bra. I found it on the pillows. *Those* pillows.

I take a step closer just to make sure I'm seeing things right. Pink T-shirt. Long hair. Long legs.

God.

There's no doubt. My stomach twists as I realize this jerk has footage of himself having sex with Lindsay at the party last weekend.

And the guy behind the camera was Bryce.

Josh and Bryce knew they were going to do this. They planned it. They'd set it all up from the start. Josh was going to nail someone, and Bryce was going to catch it on video.

And it just so happened that Lindsay was the one who rubbed herself all over Josh that evening. So she got to be the star of the show.

Who the hell does this kind of thing? What game is this?

My blood boils as I look around at these idiots. They think this video is funny.

They're loving it. They think Josh is a superstud. I want to smash my fist through the classroom window beside me. I want to smash my fist into every face in this group. And I want to take Josh and pound his head right into this ugly carpet below our feet.

But I don't. I'd get killed. There are five of them and one of me.

My jaw clenches. I back away quietly until I enter the flow of students headed to class. My blood pulses in my ears. I feel sick.

I wish I could stop what just happened. Stop Josh from showing people his stupid video. Speak up and tell him he's a bastard. That he's done something really wrong—illegal, actually. If I had the balls, I'd walk right up to him and tell him to hand the phone over to me.

But I don't do any of that.

I'm too mad to think straight. So I just walk away. Feeling like a coward, but not sure what else I can do.

I crash through the double doors leading outside. I need fresh air. But the smokers are standing right there at the entrance, and instead of grabbing a breath of $O_2$ I suck in a bunch of airborne carcinogens that other people have breathed out. Nice.

I duck back inside. I need to think.

Should I tell someone? Should I call the counselor? Or the principal? Should I tell a teacher? Or maybe the nurse. She would be the best place to start. Wouldn't she? Maybe I should just go straight to the cops. Josh and Bryce have definitely crossed the line. And even though her hair covers her face in the video, I can prove it's Lindsay. It was the same bed. The same bra.

The same body.

The next question hits me like a ton of bricks: Should I tell Lindsay? It's her right to know that this video is out there. But what good would it do to tell her? It would hurt her, no doubt. Shock her. Make her even more ashamed when she's already feeling like a skank.

No. I decide I can't tell Lindsay. There's nothing she can do about it now. It would kill her to know about this. What she doesn't know won't hurt her. Josh sure isn't going to tell her about it. Why would he? He'd get in huge trouble if the school or the cops ever found out.

But what if the video gets out? And what if people somehow found out it was Lindsay? She'd never live it down.

My head hurts.

My only option is to get that phone away from Josh. If I could somehow scoop it, then I could delete the footage and slip the phone back to him. He wouldn't even know the difference until he looked for the video again. And then he'd probably figure he just deleted it by accident.

I like this idea. I head back toward the lockers, turning it over in my mind. Yeah, that's what I'll do. I'll boost his phone from his bag when he's not looking.

I turn the corner back into the hallway. I'm relieved to be taking action.

The crowd has dispersed. I watch Josh hit a button on his phone. He's still grinning. The screen goes dark. He slips the phone into the front pocket of his jeans.

No way I'm getting that phone now.

And just like that, my great idea falls to pieces.

## Chapter Twelve

After school, I fly home on my bike. I need to think things through. I need to figure out how to stop that video from being shown to anyone else. I also want to make sure Josh gets his ass kicked. Hard. So that he doesn't do this again.

At home, I sling my schoolbag onto a hook and head to my mom's office.

She's good to talk to. She might have some thoughts.

I stick my head around the doorframe. "Hey. I'm home."

Mom looks over from her monitor. Some complicated map of heat zones under the ocean. Geothermal something-or-other. She's been working at home for as long as I can remember. After I was born, she decided she didn't want to work in an office downtown. She wanted to be there for me when I came home from school. And she always is.

"Hey, baby," she says.

Out of old habit, I check in with her every day. I usually just say hi and then go upstairs and find something to eat. But today I stick around.

I flop onto the big green chair that's just inside her door. It's a small office— barely enough room for a desk, armchair and a printer table.

Mom takes off her glasses and turns her chair to face me. She knows when something's bugging me. "How was school?"

"Could've been better," I say. "Didn't see a physics quiz coming." I examine my knuckles for a few moments.

Mom waits.

"Can I get your opinion on something?" I ask.

She leans back in her chair. "Shoot."

"Remember when I went to Erin's party last weekend?" I begin.

She nods. "I do."

"Well, things got a little weird. Some crazy stuff happened." I back up and sketch out some background on how Lindsay changed over the summer. How she's been so different since the start of school. Then I tell her about how I watched Lindsay get really loaded at the party. And drop. And disappear into a bedroom with two guys.

Of course, I explain my attempts to intervene too. But even as I say the words, it comes out sounding so lame. I wish I'd done more.

"And today I saw Josh in the hallway by the seniors' lockers," I finish. "He has it all on camera, Mom. He was showing a whole bunch of his friends. He had his buddy Bryce record it for him. That's why two of them went into the room. One guy to mess around with Lindsay. And another guy to catch it on his camera phone." I run my hands through my hair. Just thinking about Josh and his stupid friends gets me all steamed again.

"So what did you do after you realized he has this video?" my mother asks.

It's the question I've been dreading. I don't have an answer. At least, I don't have the right answer—or one that feels right to me.

"I thought about telling the school counselor, or the nurse," I say.

"But it almost feels like I'd be telling on Linds, you know?" I shake my head. "I thought about going to the cops. But then she'll be mad at me forever." I let out a long sigh. "I thought about taking Josh's phone too. Except he keeps it in his jeans. I can't steal it from in there."

"Have you told Lindsay yet? About the video?"

"No. And that's what I wanted to ask you," I say. "Do you think I should? I was thinking it wouldn't do her any good to know. I mean, she can't do anything about it. And it would just make her feel worse than she already does."

Mom nods. She's quiet for a moment. She clears her throat and speaks slowly, like she does when she's thinking things through. "I think—since you're asking my opinion—that you should tell Lindsay first," she says. "Before you go to anyone else."

"Really?" I totally didn't figure on this answer. "Why? What good is that going to do?"

"Well, you've told me Lindsay's kind of been getting out of control, right?"

I nod.

"But even so," she continues, "she's the only person who can be responsible for her own body and behavior. It's not up to you or anyone else to look after her."

I consider this.

"Don't get me wrong," she says. "It's good that you're looking out for her. I know how much she means to you. You two have always been good friends. And Lindsay's going through a hard time." Mom pauses. "But she needs a wake-up call, Mike, before things get any worse for her. I like Lindsay, and I wouldn't want to see her get hurt by this either. You owe it to her to tell her about the video. And she owes it to herself to start taking responsibility for her actions."

"But what about Josh?" I burst out. "Shouldn't *he* be responsible for his actions?" I can feel my ears growing hot.

Mom shrugs. "That's up to Lindsay to decide. She's got to be the one to take control of this situation." She puts her glasses back on and looks at me. "I'm not saying that this is the way it has to be, Mike. But you asked me for my opinion. And now you have it."

She's right. I asked.

I stand. "I don't know," I say. "I gotta think about this some more."

"You do that, baby. Good luck with it," she says, turning her attention back to her screen. "Let me know how it all turns out."

"I will."

I think about my mom's words as I head to work. She's probably right. This is Lindsay's mess.

The newspaper warehouse is hot. I'm sweating within minutes. I stop after a few dozen bundles and swipe my arm across my forehead. I decide to tell Lindsay tomorrow that she's got to go to the police. Mom's right: she's the one who should do it. I'll stand behind her and support her every inch of the way. But she's got to be the one to start that conversation.

I feel better. The knot in my stomach loosens a bit. I'm finally going to do something to help my best friend.

But even so, it doesn't feel like enough. I'm furious with Josh and Bryce. I still feel like I should do something to fix what they've done.

# Chapter Thirteen

I pull Lindsay aside at lunch the next day. Literally. As she leaves the school with Renata and Erin, I grab her elbow. "We have to talk," I say. I steer her toward a bench near the parking lot.

I sit. She doesn't.

She stands in front of me, arms crossed. "What's this about, Mike?" Her voice is hard. So are her eyes. It's such a change from the other night, when she was telling me how crushed she felt when she found me and Scarlett on the swing. To look at her now, you'd think I was something she couldn't wipe off her shoes.

Whatever. I'm not here to talk about how she feels about me.

"Sit down, Linds. This is serious."

She narrows her eyes. She doesn't like me telling her what to do. But she also knows whatever I have to say must be important enough for me to have dragged her away from her friends.

She gives an irritated little sigh and perches on the edge of the bench. "Happy now?"

I ignore her bitchy tone. "You have to go to the police about what happened at the party."

Lindsay looks like I've just slapped her. She takes a second before she responds. "What are you talking about?" Her voice is frosty.

"You know what I'm talking about," I say. "I was there."

I wish I didn't have to be having this conversation. But she has to know.

"Josh has a video of it on his camera phone, Linds." I speak quietly. "Bryce took it the night of the party."

She stares at me for a long moment. "What?" she whispers. Her eyes are huge, disbelieving. Suddenly the Ice Queen facade drops away, and I'm looking at the Lindsay I know. She sucks in a breath and turns away from me. Closes her eyes.

I don't say anything. What can I possibly say that will make things better?

"How do you know?" she whispers.

I pause. "Josh was showing the video to a few guys on his phone yesterday," I say. "By his locker."

She leans forward, elbows on her knees. Covers her face with her hands. I want to touch her. Rub her back or something, but I don't know if it's what she would want.

"Did you…see it all? Mike? Did you watch it?"

I shake my head. "No. I didn't," I say quietly. "I left. I was too angry."

"How do you know it was me?" Her voice is barely a whisper.

God. I have to explain? "I saw your…your bra," I say. "The pink one. That's how I knew it was you." She flinches, and I hurry to reassure her. "But that's the only way I knew, Linds. No one else could possibly figure it out. Your hair was covering your face. It's impossible to tell that it's you." Suddenly I feel incredibly awkward.

Lindsay presses her palms to her forehead. A sob escapes her lips.

"Linds, I'm so sorry." I let the silence settle for a minute.

She doesn't move. I take a deep breath and carry on. "What Josh did was illegal. Drugging you. Taking advantage of you. Filming you. And now showing it to other people."

The color drains from her face as I talk.

"You need to report it, Linds."

She's silent for a moment. Then she straightens. She doesn't look at me. When she speaks, the chill has crept back into her voice. "I don't think so, Mike."

"What? Why not?"

"It wouldn't go over very well."

I can't believe what I'm hearing. "Who cares how it goes over? The guy committed a crime, Lindsay. Against *you*. You need to report it to the police. You can't let him get away with this."

Lindsay turns on me with eyes that could cut steel. In one vicious movement, she shoves me, hard. I lurch backward and almost fall off the bench.

"What the hell?" I gasp, grabbing at the backrest to keep my balance.

"Shut up, Mike," she hisses. "Just shut up, okay? You don't know what you're saying. You don't know what you're telling me to do."

Suddenly I'm angry too. This conversation makes no sense.

"What do you mean, I don't know what I'm saying?" I say. "A guy you barely know has footage of you having sex with him and you're just going to stand by and…and…let him show it around?" I realize I'm nearly shouting. "To the whole school?"

Lindsay's eyes flash. "You don't get it." She shakes her head like she can't believe how stupid I am. "Fine. So Josh got it on camera. Do you realize what will happen to me if I go to the police about it, Mike? Huh? Do you have any clue?" She spits the words at me. "No, you don't. Because *you don't get it*." She looks away, then back at me. "Here. Let me lay it out for you." Her voice is low and cold. "If I rat him out to the cops, this whole thing will blow up in my face. They'll drag Josh and his friend in for statements. And me. And a ton of other people. Renata. Sara. Erin. Anyone who was at the party. It'll get out, Mike, and everyone will know it's me in the video."

My head spins as I try to sort out her words. "Rat him out? You say it like you're the one who's doing the wrong thing," I say. "But he should be charged, Linds. He *assaulted* y—"

She cuts me off, furious. "Yeah, Mike, I'd be bringing Josh up on charges. Great. Reporting the king of Westpark High to the police." She gives a bitter laugh. "Don't you understand what will happen? Everybody will turn against me. I won't have any friends left." She crosses her arms and legs, drawing herself tight. She looks away for a moment. "Josh is the most popular guy in the whole school. I'm a zero compared to him. Who's going to take my side? My friends will drop me like a diseased rodent." She gestures in frustration. "Even if people realize what Josh did was wrong, they're too chickenshit to hold it against him. People always blame the victim."

I shake my head, even though I know at least part of what she's saying is true. "No, they don't," I say. "Not necessarily. This is different."

Her look stops me from saying anything else.

She's right.

It's so unfair. But she's right.

If this gets out, she'll be destroyed.

But what the hell am I *saying*? Josh committed a crime. And here we are, tripping on the realization of how hard it will be to make him pay for it. It's so much easier to walk away and not create any ripples. But that's so *wrong*. That asshole should pay for what he did to Lindsay.

"Linds," I say. "I'll stand by you." I reach over and take her hand in mine. "You know that. You need to turn Josh in. You can't let him get away with this."

"Yeah?" Her gray eyes snap angrily. "Easy for you to say."

I sigh. "It might not be as bad as you think."

She pulls her hand out of mine. "Look, forget about it, Mike. Okay?" Her voice wavers. "Just…move on."

"Linds." I go to take her hand again. "Hey."

Wrong move.

"Stop it. Just stop it!" Suddenly her voice breaks, and she's crying. "Just leave me alone. I don't know why you even care. Have you forgotten what you walked in on last Friday?" She wipes her eyes with the backs of her hands. "I'm not who you think I am, Mike. I'm not the perfect little Lindsay you used to know. Little Miss Gymnastics, Little Miss A-plus Student, Little Miss Never-Slept-With-A-Guy. That girl's *gone*." She fights for control, her breath hitching and her voice rising as the words rush out in a blaze of anger. "She's long gone, Mike, and she's not ever coming back. And I don't know what you'd want with a dirty slut like me. So stop wasting your time."

A wrenching sob follows and then she's on her feet, hands over her face, stumbling away. From the bench, from the school. From the video that could completely trash her reputation at Westpark High.

From me.

# Chapter Fourteen

On Thursday, I arrive at school to find the worst has happened. The video has gone viral throughout the school. People are talking about it. Texting about it. Forwarding it to each other. Huddling in little groups in the field, watching it on their phones and iPods. The teachers are clueless; what else is new.

Everyone's trying to figure out who it is. Names are flying, but none stick. I'm glad for Lindsay's sake they can't identify her. They can't tell who the guy is either. Josh and his buddies must be locked up on that. He's smart. He knows enough not to let himself be identified.

I pass a group of people whispering near the locker room. I wonder if Lindsay has seen the video yet, or if she's avoiding it. She's avoiding me, there's no doubt about that. Every time I saw her yesterday she turned and headed in a different direction.

Now I'm faced with a choice. The video is public. I have direct proof that Josh assaulted Lindsay. I have enough to take it to the police, whether she wants me to or not.

I want to see this jerk fry.

But then I think of how Lindsay said it would destroy her if the cops got hold of it.

It's a pretty raw deal. Making it with Josh at the party would have been something to talk about. Shag 'n' brag. Her friends would envy her for that. One more notch in her belt. A big one.

But now that there's actual video footage of her little party trick…that changes everything. Whether it's fair or not. There's a fine line between hooking up with a popular guy…and becoming a Paris Hilton porn star. And unfortunately—with Bryce's thoughtful help—Lindsay crossed that line without even knowing it.

She's right. With this footage, the whole game changes. She'll be labeled a whore once people find out it's her. The worst part? After the initial gossip dies down, Josh will be more popular than ever. It's like some sick cosmic joke. He'll be the stud, she'll be the slut, and the world will continue to spin.

I skip my last class to think.

It's a tough call. I want to take this to the cops. I want that scumbag to be busted wide-open for what he did to Lindsay. I want him to pay a big ugly fine, or do a few years in jail, or pull some heavy community service or whatever they do with creeps that film themselves screwing girls at parties.

But like Lindsay says, if this goes to the cops, they're going to want evidence. All kinds of statements from people. It'll get out. And it'll wreck her reputation, which is impossible to recover from. She'll have to move schools. And even then she might not get away from it. It's so frustrating. I'm beginning to understand how hard it is for girls who find themselves in situations like this. Their choices are limited to Bad or Worse.

But I can't just do *nothing*. If he doesn't get busted for this, Josh could easily take advantage of some other girl.

And who's to say his friends won't start doing it too—especially if they know they won't get caught?

I can't let him get away with it.

But if I turn him in, Lindsay's reputation will be killed—and so will our friendship. She'll see this as the ultimate betrayal. I will lose her forever.

But if I don't do something…I might lose her anyway. The last thing she said to me on Tuesday before she stormed off. That bit about how she's a slut. She's going to start to believe it. I'm worried she's just going to get worse. More drinking. More drugs. More sex.

More of what she never stood for.

I think back to Tuesday's conversation. I see Lindsay's point. She can't go to the cops without this whole thing coming apart at the seams. But I don't want her world to fall apart either.

I decide to take matters into my own hands.

## Chapter Fifteen

I don't have to go to the police. I don't have to blow this whole thing wide-open. I can deal with this myself.

At least I can try.

It scares the hell out of me, but I can confront Josh about the video.

The last bell has rung, and students are pouring out of the main doors. I know where to find Josh. He'll be hanging around the portables out back. He and his little band of emo drama freaks like to hang out there after school. Maybe they read Chaucer and Yeats. Smoke up and challenge each other to fake duels. I don't know.

I decide to go now, before I can chicken out. My heart is racing and I have to keep wiping my palms on my jeans. I try to think about what I'm going to say.

I spot him leaning against the railing of the stairs to one of the portables. He's alone. I'm glad. I still have no idea how I'm going to handle things.

As I approach, I realize how tall he is. Much bigger than me. That's okay. I'm not going to be intimidated by him. *I'm* the athlete, not him. He might beat me in a Shakespeare smackdown, but I'd kick his ass in the gym any day.

Josh looks up. I give him the faintest of nods. I don't know how to negotiate this kind of thing, so I just plow in.

"Pretty crazy video that's going around, eh?" I say.

He studies me coolly. "What video is that?"

"I think you know the one," I say. "It involves you. And a very drunk girl at a party."

He's trying to look like he has no idea what I'm talking about. I expected as much.

I push on. Right now it's just the two of us, and I don't know how long I have until his buddies arrive.

"I know you're behind it," I continue. "You and your friend Bryce."

Josh narrows his eyes. "What are you talking about?"

I force myself to keep an even tone. "I'm talking about last Friday's party, Josh. When you and your friend took a girl—and your camera phone—into the bedroom. She was drunk and high. Remember that? Or have you forgotten?"

I reach into my pocket and pull out my cell phone. "Want me to refresh your memory? I have it right here. As does pretty much every other person in the entire school."

Josh looks at me for a moment. Then he smirks. "I've seen the chick in that video," he says. "Looks like a nice little piece. But I don't know anything about it."

"I think you know quite a bit about it," I say. "And guess what? What you did is illegal." I drop my voice. "Could cause you some ugly trouble if you were ever to be brought up on charges."

His expression doesn't change. He's good at this acting thing.

"Why would I be charged?" he says. Smooth as silk. "There's no proof that it's me. Nobody knows who either of those people are in the video."

I shake my head. It's my turn to smile. "That 'nice little piece'?

She's my best friend. And I'm the one who put her back together once you guys left the party."

Josh's smile falters a bit.

I spot my opening and go in for the kill.

But I don't get the chance. As I open my mouth to tell him I'm going to the cops with it, he lunges at me. I'm not expecting it. He comes at me from the third stair, catlike, knocking me flat on the concrete. Before I can roll out from under him, his fist slams into the side of my face. Things go black on that side for a few seconds. Blurry on the other.

I bring my hands together and smash them across his neck. He grunts and swoops backward, catching himself before he hits the pavement. I roll to the side and take another hit to the face. I roll again, twice, to get away from him and gather my legs under me. Something warm drips into my mouth.

I spit. Blood.

More comes. I spit again.

Then I'm up, charging at him like some kind of deranged bull. I've never been in a fight before. All I know is that I want to take this guy out. I want to win. I want to have the last word.

The top of my head connects with the center of his chest. I can almost see the *POW!* in bold zap lettering, like something out of a Batman comic.

Josh's feet actually leave the ground. He flies backward, crashing against the side of a black pickup truck. He grabs at the mirror but misses and slides to the ground. Then I'm on top of him, pinning him against the door. Gripping the bottom half of his face with my hand.

I sit on his knees to stop him from getting up.

Josh's hands grab my wrist, trying to pull my hand away from his face. But I won't let him. I hook my finger and thumb around the back of his jaw. If he pulls my hand off, the lower half of his skull is coming with it.

I whack the back of his head into the truck a couple of times. Just to get his attention. He groans. There's nothing else he can do. He can't talk, because my hand's clamping his jaws shut.

I lean in nice and close so he can hear me.

"You get seven years for sexual assault, Josh," I say. "I'm almost *sure* you weren't planning on spending any time in the can after graduation. Aren't you gunning for that nice theater program in New York?" He grows still. His eyes lock on mine, huge and bloodshot. "What you did to Lindsay could destroy her reputation at this school," I continue. "Not only that, but it's against the law. I'm ready to go to the police with this, and Lindsay is totally prepared to press charges. Plenty of people saw you guys leaving that room at the party."

I'm bluffing with this last bit, but Josh won't know any different.

"So," I say. "You wanna hear what I think you should do?"

He nods. He might have whimpered too, but I can't be sure.

"Good. Here's what I think you should do. I think that video should just die a quiet death. Without you ever breathing a word about who's in it. Stop spreading it. And most importantly, don't even think of doing that to a girl ever again. That shit wrecks people's lives, Josh." I give his head another smack against the truck. "You feeling me?"

Josh groans again. Nods.

"You're not going to make me go to the cops on this, Josh, are you?"

*Whack.*

Josh shakes his head.

"Atta boy." I stare at him for a long moment. Then I give him an extra little push and let go. Suddenly free, Josh grabs his jaw with both hands and moans.

I stand up, resisting a childish urge to kick him.

Instead I turn and walk away without looking back.

# Chapter Sixteen

I swing my leg over my bike and start to pedal.

My head is buzzing with all this stuff. My world has been turned upside down in a matter of days. Lindsay has pretty much confessed that she's into me—and has been for just as long as I've been into her. But she's so messed up. She's angry and out of control.

Her life is in a monster spiral. She's got naked pictures of herself being spread all around the Internet.

And I've just beat the crap out of the guy who's responsible.

Everything looks very different than it did a week ago. Life is weird like that.

I decide I'll head to Lindsay's house. I'll tell her something she'll want to hear: that Josh has promised never to let it slip about it being her in the video. She'll be relieved not to have to go to the police—even though I would prefer that she did. I want him to pay for what he did.

Although I guess I did make him pay just now. Just a little bit. I'm looking forward to telling Lindsay about my little meet-up with Josh.

As I rip along the streets, another more important thought hits me: I still haven't told her anything about how I really feel. About her. I've been meaning to, but I just haven't found the right time. She has yet to hear the words from me that she's probably needing to hear right about now.

That she's been needing to hear for, like, months.

As far as I know, Lindsay has no idea that I'm in love with her.

I pedal faster. As I race toward her house, I imagine how great everything is going to be when I finally tell her how I feel.

When I get to her place, I knock. It feels weird. Before things fell apart, I used to just go straight inside.

No one comes.

I wait for a few more seconds and knock again. Still no answer. I glance at my phone. It's 4:18 PM. Lindsay's dad is still at work. Her mother is probably out shopping. Lorraine loves her afternoons at the mall.

I open the front door.

"Linds?" I call. I know she's home. Her car is in the driveway.

No answer. Maybe she's on the computer downstairs. I go and look, but she's not there.

Maybe she's got the laptop in her bedroom.

That's where I find her. But she's not on the laptop. She's in bed, asleep. Wow, she must be really burned out from all this stress, I realize. She's had a brutal week.

I sit on the side of the bed, feeling nervous. Which is dumb, because how many times have we sat together on this bed and worked on projects? How many times have we studied for tests here?

I reach a hand out and gently stroke her shoulder. "Linds," I say. "It's me."

She doesn't move. I shake her a bit. "Linds." A few strands of hair have fallen over her face and I tuck them behind her ear. "Linds, wake up."

But she doesn't.

Suddenly I'm filled with a bad feeling.

I pull back the covers. She's fully clothed.

Then I see the empty medicine container in her hand.

No.

I grab the plastic jar and turn it around until I can see the label. Lorazepam. Lindsay told me her mother is afraid of flying. I'm holding her bottle of tranquilizers for when she travels.

It's a big container. And it's empty.

"No!" I shout. I give Lindsay a hard shake, enough to flop her head off the pillow, but she's unresponsive. I stare wildly around for the phone before remembering I have my cell with me. I snatch it out of my pocket and dial 9-1-1.

The dispatcher listens as I fluster through explaining the situation. He takes the address and tells me that an ambulance will arrive within six minutes. His voice is flat. Calm. Maybe he figures that's reassuring to people who are losing it.

Like me.

"Is there a suicide note?" Flat-Voice Man asks me. "Any message you can see?"

I stare around. The word *suicide* ricochets around inside my head. Suicide? Are we really talking about suicide? What the *hell*?

I look on the bedside table. Under the covers. Under the pillow. On the floor. The dresser. The bathroom. The kitchen.

Nothing.

"No, nothing," I gasp. I feel the tears threatening to overtake me. "There's no note."

She meant every bit of this.

## Chapter Seventeen

The ambulance comes. Damned if I'm not going to ride along with Lindsay. The paramedics are fine with it.

I sit as close as I can to her, holding her hand. As I watch her chest rise and fall, I start making bargains. *Please, God, if you're out there, don't take her away from me. Please. I'll do whatever it takes. Just make sure she's okay.*

*I'll work hard in school. I'll help Mom more. I'll be so good to Lindsay.*

I hate that this has happened. I hate that I didn't leave school right away to go to Lindsay's place. But then, I had to take care of Josh. And I was so ready to tell Lindsay all about it. I had no idea what she was thinking. How bad things had gotten.

What if I had arrived ten minutes later? I shudder and look out the rear windows.

It's started to rain.

Like my heart, the streets are cold and empty as we fly toward the hospital, siren screaming.

As soon as we roll to a stop, the doors open and Lindsay is wheeled out by two waiting attendants. The paramedics hop down and help. They whisk her off through the sliding doors and down a corridor, out of sight.

A nurse tells me she'll need to have her stomach pumped.

She's little, this nurse. Mom's age. Tight-lipped, but warm. Her nametag says *Joanne*. She holds her clipboard precisely and asks me a million questions about Lindsay. Has she tried to commit suicide before? Whose drugs were they? Did her mother use drugs often? What happened to make Lindsay want to harm herself?

I answer most of the nurse's questions honestly. But I lie and tell her I don't know any reason why she would take the pills. That's for Lindsay to talk about. If she makes it.

*When* she makes it. I'm not going to believe that she's not going to make it.

I wonder how she's going to be feeling when she comes around.

Will she be pissed to find herself still here? Will she be mad at me for pulling her back from the Big Sleep?

Will she want to see me?

Joanne's voice jerks me back to earth. She's all business. "A social worker is on his way," she tells me.

I nod.

"Do you have phone numbers for Lindsay's parents? The social worker will want to speak with them," she says.

Of course. I have to call Lorraine and Darius. They'll be arriving home anytime now, wondering where their daughter is. They need to know what's happening.

"Uh, yeah," I say. "I'll give them a call."

"Good." The nurse tucks her pen back into the little metal clasp on her clipboard. Her face softens. She touches my arm. "She'll be okay, Michael. She came in early enough."

Tears sting my eyes and I nod again. "Good," I say. A huge weight edges itself off my chest. "Thanks."

She smiles.

Part of me desperately wants to believe what the nurse said. That Lindsay's going to make it.

But another part is terrified she's never coming back.

I realize I don't know Darius's number at work. I don't know Lorraine's cell number either. Suddenly I panic.

I force myself to take a deep breath.

Well, duh, Mike.

I can call my mom and have her get ahold of Lindsay's parents.

"Mom?" I say when she picks up. I'm careful to control my voice.

"Hey, sweetie. Where are you? You're usually home by now."

"Yeah. Well, I'm at the hospital," I say.

Mom's voice sharpens. "What's wrong? Michael? Honey? Are you all right?"

"Yes. Yeah. I'm okay, Mom," I reassure her. "I'm okay. But Lindsay's sick. I, uh…I brought her here." With a bit of help.

"Oh," she says. I can hear the relief in her voice. "Well, is she going to be all right? What's she sick with?"

And then I explain. All of it. Every bit.

"Oh, honey," Mom says when I finish. "I'm sure she's getting the best care possible." She's probably right. And it's what I need to hear. "Lindsay's been through a lot this year. You've been a good friend to her, Michael."

Have I? I'm not so sure.

I shake my head. "Not good enough," I say. "But I'm here for her now."

As I put the words out there, I realize they're totally correct. I *am* here now.

Fully. Fearlessly. Finally.

"Hey, listen, Mom. Can you call Lindsay's folks? I don't have their numbers. They need to know what happened."

"You bet, baby," she says. "I'll let them know she's stable. They'll want to come down right away."

"Kay. Thanks."

"Mike?"

"Yeah?"

"Do you want me to come down there too?"

I think about this. But there's nothing my mother can do. Soon enough I'll have Lindsay's parents to talk to. And the social worker. And the nurses. Maybe doctors.

But first I want to see Lindsay.

"Nah," I say. "I think I'm okay. I won't be home until later though."

"Fine, baby," says Mom. "Take care of you."

"Take care of you," I say back. I send the same words to Lindsay.

I close my phone and sit on the curb for a few minutes to pull myself together.

When I head back through the sliding doors, the nurse informs me that Lindsay's been admitted. Room 262. I head for the stairs.

As I get there, a doctor is leaving the room. She's short, and her glasses sit far down on her nose. "Are you the one who brought this young lady in?" she asks. She peers at me over the top of her glasses. Everything about her says *smart*. And a lot says *tired*.

I nod.

"You're her boyfriend?"

I shrug. "Something like that." When I say the words, a little tribe of butterflies suddenly breaks loose in my stomach. I could get used to that feeling.

I nod toward the closed door. "How is she?"

She sighs. "She'll be fine," she says. "She's a very lucky young woman. There were a lot of drugs in her system."

I shudder. I'm not going to let myself think about what might have happened.

"She needs to rest," the doctor continues. "I'll let you have a few moments with her, and then I'd like to talk with you about what happened."

I nod. "Okay. Thanks."

She swishes away, soft-soled shoes squeaking on the waxed floors. I'm left standing in front of the wide blue door. It's the only thing standing between me and the future.

I stare down at my hand on the doorknob.

And turn.

Alex Van Tol makes her living as a word ninja in Victoria, British Columbia. She writes for businesses and magazines, and spends way too much time online. *Viral* is Alex's third novel with Orca Book Publishers. Get to know her better at alexvantol.com.